DIS
TRAC TION

a critical
look at life
in the
screen age

BY TJ PROSIT

DISTRACTION

TJ PROSIT

ILLUSTRATIONS AND COVER DESIGN BY
MARIELLE FREDERICK

TABLE OF CONTENTS

Preface

What motivated me to write this book was the hope that I might help each of us break through the stimulation clouds all around that may be distracting us from the much more important job of living a life more awake and aware, a life that is the very best of what we have to offer for our own benefit and those in our care. My hope is that this book will shine at least one small light on what I see happening with growing intensity. It doesn't take a degree in sociology or Blue-Ribbon panel of experts to see what is happening right in front of us.

Every single person on this planet has been given unique gifts and talents to benefit themselves, their families, and their communities. The impact we can have varies from person to person. As in a play, some are directors, some play a leading role, some supporting roles, some handle staging, some provide costuming, etc. No one role can carry the performance and every job is critical to the ultimate success. And as the performance comes to an end, the applause is for all those who played a part, large or small, who didn't let the distractions get in the way of the best production possible.

Before I go on, I don't write this from the standpoint of a sociologist or from any other scientific background. As did most who attended high school, college, or university, I did take classes in sociology and psychology, but I have no special degree in the field.

And while I have read various books on history, culture, religion, philosophy, and more, I have no degrees in any of these fields either. My education focus was in business, marketing, and economics and my career has been in various aspects of marketing with a focus on performance improvement and employee reward programs designed to encourage and reward productive work. Successful programs require being a student of human behavior and motivations. As a father of three wonderful and very talented now adult children, I have seen the positive impact on my own children and other kids in our community who were active and encouraged to learn and explore and the many and varied qualities, talents, and skills they developed.

A country and its culture cannot survive long unless every citizen makes it a self- appointed duty to be productive, to find a personal potential, to take the gifts given to them and nurture and grow those gifts for their own benefit and the extended benefit to their family and then to their community. Put another way, I think most would agree that we all must be good stewards of the planet's natural resources. Well then, isn't it a reasonable analogy that we should each be good stewards of our personal resources? Our talents and gifts are our personal natural resources that deserve good stewardship.

Chapter 1: My "A-ha" moment

As I think back, what started me thinking about this subject began years ago listening to a radio program featuring a panel of college professors and business professionals talking about the quality of students entering and graduating from U.S. universities and colleges. The professors were noting that a growing number of college freshmen were requiring remedial assistance in basic subjects. More recently, a 2013 USA Today article reported that 1 in 5 college freshman required remedial educational assistance. These are students who graduated high school presumably completing all required courses yet arriving for freshman year of college needing remedial assistance in English, math and other basic subjects. And just to be clear, I don't believe this is a reflection on the intelligence or capability of any of those students.

Similarly, from that same panel discussion, business owners were concerned about basic business knowledge, social skills, and simply a readiness to work upon graduation. Another survey mirrored this same opinion. From Slate.com February 2014...In a new survey by Gallup measuring how business leaders and the American public view the state and value of higher education, just 14 percent of Americans—and only 11 percent of business leaders—strongly agreed that (college) graduates have the necessary skills and competencies to succeed in the workplace.

Granted, this is only a measure of academic and business acumen, but I start here for a reason. Today and every day moving forward, we will require the services of many men and women performing various tasks and producing various products using skills with at least some foundation learned in high school, trade schools, or college. Each of the services or products have varying degrees of importance, immediacy, and significance to us and require varied types and duration of education to master.

When we wake up in the morning and flip the light switch in the bathroom, we expect the light to come on. When we turn on the shower, we expect hot water to come out thanks to that new water heater installed by people who we assume are professionals. We hope the new body wash is just as invigorating as it seemed on the commercial. We expect that the tube of toothpaste is free of any nasty bacteria. On the more serious side, we might be hoping the minor surgery planned for later today goes well. And many of us expect that the train conductor on the commuter line is more focused on a safe run than texting a buddy about last night's baseball game. I could go on, but you get the idea.

We tend to take all these things for granted, but everything from your local electric provider to the personal goods manufacturer to your medical care requires people doing a job well. And keep in mind, almost all the work and attention to detail is done completely voluntarily. If you think about it, other than those under extremely close supervision, very few employees are compelled at any moment to do a job well. It is our collective expectation that various services will be properly performed and correctly executed. If we are to live our lives in any degree of order, that is how every day must be. And that goes for what WE are doing every day as well. Without people with various skills performing them well, or at least proficiently, many parts of everyday life begin to fall apart.

How long should we expect all those various services will continue to be provided effectively and with professionalism when only 11 percent of business people believe college grads are ready to work?   Even those established in the workforce have challenges with surveys saying that up to 70 percent of employees are "disengaged" at work. Every job, every service needs to be performed well by a person accepting all the responsibilities of that job for a community and society to function.

What a difference it would make if each of us focused our energies on exploring our potential and attending to our responsibilities. How might our lives be made better if we could clearly see what is tugging and pulling at our attention and keeping us from enriching our minds during those education years, doing our jobs to our very best ability, being loyal spouses and attentive parents, enriching our minds, exploring our gifts. A culture can only maintain a way of life and the liberty to enjoy it if we are all fully awake and aware and participating with a sense of responsibility.

The possibilities are endless, but it must start with

recognizing and clearing away that which is useless and harmful.

Chapter 2: What Is Distraction?

Have you ever been watching a TV program while a boiling pot overflows on the stove? How about reading some tabloid cover in the rack at the grocery store line and not realizing the line has moved up?   And who hasn't been trying to get a school project done while letting your mind wander only to realize two hours later you have made no progress whatsoever.

We all have a pretty good idea of what distraction means and have experienced it in our lives to one degree or another, but for clarity, let's look at a few formal definitions.

Webster's first definition is:

  The act of distracting or state of being distracted, especially mental confusion.

The first definition I found on a web search says:

  A thing that prevents someone from giving full attention to something else.

But I think the definition from the Online Psychology Dictionary best fits my message of this book, which is:

An interruption to attention or anything that draws attention away from a primary task.

I'm going to come back to this definition again, but it's those last words "primary task" that should be on your mind throughout this book.

 Whichever definition we use and relate to, we have all experienced distraction in our lives, and I put myself solidly in the middle of that group.

All of us also know that sometimes distractions are exactly what we need to take a mental break from the many stresses of life, so let's agree some types of distraction can be beneficial. However, some distraction can be quite literally deadly.

We hear about the serious issue of distracted driving but take a minute to look at the statistics and it's likely a much bigger problem than you think. In 2013 there were 3,154 people killed because of distracted driving. And in 2015 1.3M crashes on U.S. highways were a result of texting while driving.

Deborah A. P. Hersman, as president and CEO of The National Safety Council in 2014, said that in their research they found cell phones were a factor in 27 percent of accidents and that 61 percent of drivers surveyed admit they text while driving. AT&T research seemed to back that up, indicating that about 70 percent of smart phone users are on the phone while driving, prompting the "It Can Wait" campaign.

But what if instead of driving alone in a car, the distracted person is responsible for hundreds of people? It was just another train run, one that happened in Chatsworth, California on a regular schedule, but on this day in 2013 it would turn deadly. The driver on duty and in control of the train was on his phone, texting. While he was focused on the back and forth messaging, he missed a critical stop sign. That missed stop sign would ultimately result in a horrible collision with a freight train and the deaths of 25, with another 135 injured. And this wasn't the only train accident in recent years with a very similar fact pattern. These events make it very clear that for people who have the responsibility of other people's lives in their hands, distraction is literally deadly serious.

And what about terrible events which are the result of inactions from ordinary citizens brought on by distraction? San Franciscans were shocked and stunned over an apparently random killing where a man shot and killed another man for no apparent reason. It might have been prevented had people in the immediate area been paying more attention. Moments before the event, the shooter was seen on a public camera on a crowded train. The camera clearly showed him taking out a .45-caliber pistol repeatedly, yet none of the dozen people around him noticed because they were focused on their personal electronic devices.

"These weren't concealed movements-- the gun is very clear," said District Attorney George Gascón. "These people are in very close proximity with him, and nobody sees this. They're just so engrossed, texting and reading and whatnot. They're completely oblivious (to) their surroundings."

The consequences of distraction in these situations are clear, immediate, and tragic. Yet, as tragic as these accidents and events are, there is a much larger and broader impact of distraction growing right in front of us and it's creeping into our lives more and more each day.

You have probably heard the curious factoid that if you throw a frog into a pot of hot water it will jump out immediately, but if you put a frog in a cool pot and warm it gradually it will stay in the pot and eventually boil to death. Yes, it's a harsh example but true. Of course, we think to ourselves, well sure, it's a frog and it doesn't have the intelligence to understand and anticipate the eventual consequences of the ever-warming water and can't project the danger--we're so much smarter. So how can it be that dropout rates for high school students are still too high? Addiction rates to drugs and alcohol continue to rise and now most particularly to heroin and opioids. Our teens are more informed than ever, have access to more information than ever, and must understand and be able to project forward the consequences of these actions, right?

For anyone who has seen the website www.rehabs. com, the devastation to the addicts' life is obvious to the viewer, but if you asked the addict as the addiction took hold, did they see any changes, any danger, would they see the slow deterioration? The experts in addiction can help us to understand what triggers this tragic path being chosen, and there is a powerful physical and emotional mix that makes recovery an extremely difficult and complex journey, but the reality remains that drug addiction is a terrible distraction from a productive life.

If we look at this from a larger vantage point, statistics on the National Institute on Drug Abuse website from November 2014 are chilling.

Abuse of tobacco, alcohol, and illicit drugs is costly to our nation, exacting over $600 billion annually in costs related to crime, lost work productivity and healthcare.

Yes, I did write that correctly- $600 billion. Of course, the cost impact on peoples' lives has an incalculable price, but this is just one of the flames heating the pot, as it were. Does anyone believe that any of the many addicts began their drug experimentation with the intention of becoming an addict and dramatically impacting the possibility of a productive life? Did any of them consciously and deliberately desire to ignore what common sense would tell them is most certainly going to numb their minds and weaken their bodies? As smart as we are, as informed as we are, with access to virtually any bit of information we want, these statistics are still our reality here in America. Distractions, both small and innocent to large and menacing, can impact our lives and the lives of those around us. Considering some of these basic statistics, the pot is most certainly boiling.

Chapter 3: Oh, the possibilities

It's easy to see what can be accomplished when distractions are pushed aside and fully embrace our unique place in life, our primary task. We're not likely to say that Einstein was "distracted" when he came up with the theory of relativity. Or we don't think of Dorothy Day as being lost in thought as she started the Catholic Workers Movement and other social justice efforts. Do we say Martin Luther King was wasting his time on bringing attention to issues of equal justice? Was Edison distracted when the idea of the electric light bulb came to mind?

 We marvel at the accomplishments of people in many areas of life, to a great degree, because they are not distracted. They are indeed focused intensely on a very specific skill and achieving mastery to a degree that it changes the world around them or fulfills their role or critical responsibilities. And we can certainly agree that people around the world, in every culture, in every age have benefited from those people who were focused on, and dedicated to, something productive.

But we don't have to look at those who have changed the world to see value in focusing energies on a specific task at hand. Have you ever watched, I mean really watched, a mother of young children on a summer afternoon in the grocery store parking lot as she manages the four-year old and the infant in the stroller and the bags of groceries, getting her two precious little ones and six bags loaded into the minivan? Between navigating the car seats, the squirming youngsters, the busy parking lot, the heat, not to mention the appointment that she is now just barely going to make...well, you won't find a brain surgeon more focused than that mom is as she makes sure her children are properly buckled in, the food put someplace it won't spill or roll and the almost astrophysicist level time space calculations going on in her head regarding how to make it to the next appointment on time.

Or have you ever had a bad splinter, one you had to struggle to remove? Do you recall thinking of anything else other than extricating the offending shard of wood as you guided the tweezers with surgical precision to relieve you of your pain? For those of you who are parents of college age kids, consider the amazing focused concentration as you fill out all the various loan and grant forms hoping to get some financial relief?

I could go on, but you get the point that we can observe these events and small vignettes in life and see that the reason it all happens and holds together is that some people in some situations are indeed very focused, very purposeful about their lives, or at least in these moments in life. It becomes very clear when we take a moment to think of what concentration and focus produces. What would our lives be like if we consciously focused our time and energy on our most important responsibilities...as a spouse, a parent, friend, neighbor, or employee? And conversely, what things are going on in our lives every day that distract us from our personal goals, family responsibilities, professional development, impact on the community we live in?

Do we really contemplate the lost opportunities which are a result of not being focused and the contributions we could be making?

Each and every life on the planet is unique. You, the person reading this right now, have incredible value. No matter the situation, income, social status, neighborhood, none of that changes the simple fact that we are each unique and have gifts and talents as well as responsibilities also unique to us. Wherever we are in life, it is life-changing to ourselves and those in our care if we embrace this idea of having a "primary task" then to uncover, grow, and share whatever our unique gifts are and apply them to that primary task. If we embrace this, it is virtually certain we will have a full and rewarding life, both for ourselves and those around us   .

Chapter 4   A meandering detour from our potential

Something is broken and it's not the capacity of the human person. I believe every person of every age in every culture has the capacity to contribute to the rich fabric of life in a powerful and unique way. It may be a great or small thing, something that touches millions or only one very special person. Thomas Edison's many inventions, most notably the electric light bulb, changed the world forever in too many ways to list. But also consider the impact of Ann Sullivan, the woman who taught Helen Keller sign language, uncovering the rich and wonderful mind of Helen Keller, forever changing the way society looked at the blind and deaf. Ultimately both Edison and Sullivan had a profound impact by focusing on a productive use of their talent and time. But we would also agree that it would have been for naught if Edison kept all his inventions to himself on some isolated electrified island paradise. And what if Anne Sullivan didn't have the patience to stay with Helen until she finally understood what Ann was teaching her?

While there are many names we all know who have made important contributions, what about the silent millions who make each day work in the many needs of all those around us? Consider the parent caring for a special needs child every single day from infancy through to adulthood? What about the volunteer who brings food to a homebound elderly person for months on end.

My kids benefited tremendously from their mom volunteering endless hours with various school programs. One project really outdid the rest. All three of our kids participated in our local high school's musicals. These were top-shelf productions and virtually all shows would sell out every year. It was a great experience for everyone who participated, from back stage to the leading role. It was wonderful to watch as so many kids discovered talents they never realized they had. Well, for many years, my kids' mother, along with a small team of parents, would spend literally months on everything from full costume creation to fitting and sizing many of the dozens of rented costumes, being one of the few parents with excellent sewing skills. It was a huge responsibility, but when the curtain came up on opening night, all that hard work was proudly worn by the entire cast.

Then there are the countless local religious and community groups distributing food and other basic needs to the marginalized in our society. The selfless lives of people we never think about have a profound impact directly on people who so desperately need love and support.

The capacity and responsibility to be one unique thread in the complex fabric of life is in every person. And to take the analogy one step further, fabric only works because every thread has a place and serves a purpose. When threads start to be removed, the entire fabric is affected and with enough removed or degraded it's not fabric at all. Many clichés come to mind such as No man is an island , If you're not part of the solution, you're part of the problem...the list is endless. The very popular Christmas holiday classic It's a Wonderful Life makes the same point about the unknown impact of the many simple things we do for others in everyday life. What George Bailey, the main character, thought was a very ordinary and unfortunate life, in fact, touched so many all around him in simple but profound ways. He never realized the positive difference he made in his small hometown until Clarence, his guardian angel, showed George what life in Bedford Falls would have been like without him. It all comes into sharp focus in the final scene of the movie where the many people he touched came to his aid in his most desperate hour. Spoiler alert here for those who haven't seen the movie- with the Bailey home filled with friends and family, George's brother raises his glass and toasts "...To George Baily, the richest man in town." And I will keep making this point. No one else can do what you and I are here to do, but that means we must realize that we possess unique qualities no one else has and can touch the people around us like no one else can, changing the lives of those around us in a powerful and totally unique way. We are fooling ourselves if we think someone else can do it in the same way and have the same impact as each of us, because each of us is totally unique.

When you have a moment, I'd like to suggest you search YouTube for either America's Got Talent or other versions of the show and specifically search the ones identified as "...most amazing..." or "...most surprising...," etc. You will see performances that will absolutely send chills down your spine and bring tears to your eyes. In most of these cases, you will see people with such incredible talents that you will say to yourself "Why on earth aren't they already sharing this gift?"   And in almost all those cases it was because these people were afraid, told they weren't good enough or just never had the chance. As their gifts were shared on stage, it became crystal clear that these talents and gifts absolutely MUST be shared to add to the beauty of the world we live in.

Consider the performance of an Olympic athlete and the training regimen they maintain to achieve that final performance we all admire. We see the wonderful floor routine in gymnastics, the amazing physical endurance in the track and swimming events, the courage of the ski jumpers, the precision of the divers, or any of the many other events requiring various skills. Many of the competitors are only in their teens or early twenties and most have been honing their skill since childhood. We can admire the years of sacrificing so much and appreciate the pinnacle of skill they have achieved and can have some idea what was required to reach the goal of becoming an Olympic athlete. We can see the value of all that sacrifice for a chance to win a medal once every four years. If that small slice of possible success can be enough to justify all that sacrifice, why do we believe putting every effort into our life performance is any less important to the people around us every single day? Aren't there spouses, kids, parents, family and friends, employers, neighbors, and communities all counting on our Olympic effort...our very best we have to offer?

Don't we realize that our home team is cheering for us to be our best every day?

If we look around us, we know people do contribute and share gifts and talents. The bright and brilliant truth is that if you take a random sampling of children and adults from around the globe, provide an environment of love and support and get them motivated through encouragement, provide the appropriate resources, focus their energies on exploring their gifts, expose them to music, the arts, science, sports, philosophy--given time, the full array of all the expressions of intelligence and talent we know will come to life.

There is absolutely no reason to believe that God-given gifts are not in every person at every age. Those gifts may be grand or very simple. My own three children have each been blessed in many ways, including musical and artistic abilities, along with a great sense of humor and very kind hearts. You can be certain that whatever your gifts or talents are, you have them for a reason. It may be the gift of patience or understanding, excellent hand-eye coordination, a wonderful grasp of math, or a talent for managing people. The list is endless. It's up to each person to uncover them, nurture them, grow them, share them, and focus on using them to achieve that Primary Task and fill in that unique spot, take up that one very special place in the fabric of life that is waiting for you. There are few things more important, but first we must clear away the useless, the mindless and destructive things in our lives.

Chapter 5: Oh, the Possibilities

As any parent reading this knows from experience, I could share stories of any of my children, but I hope they will forgive me for focusing on this one particular story. A number of years ago I had the unique privilege of seeing our oldest daughter, a very talented violinist, participate in a challenging strings orchestra program in southern NY state called "The Allegro Orchestra," run by a passionate and talented conductor known as Mr. P. The program included a few age groups, but was not particularly a special gifted student program. This was a private program open to students in the local communities from third grade to high school seniors, and any student musician was invited to audition in the appropriate age group.

One of the key differences in this string program was that Mr. P. treated them like professional musicians, steadfast and confident in their talents and ability to perform at a high level. A simple example of his expectations was a little exercise he would do occasionally with new groups. While the students were in attendance seated in chairs arrayed in the familiar arch of an orchestra, he would ask them to reach as high as they could. While seated, they would stretch up their arms with their instrument in one hand and bows pointed upward in the other. Mr. P would urge them on with "no, higher!" at which point most would stand up, arms reaching upward. To which Mr. P would urge even stronger "No, HIGHER!" at which point a few students would stand up on their chairs, arms stretched to their limit, almost touching the ceiling with their bows. At that point he would ask, "why didn't you do that the first time I asked to reach as high as you could?" He was making a point and I know it stuck with me.

Anyone who had the pleasure of attending one of the concerts would agree that this was a very special program. One particular concert was performed by the older group at Steinway Hall, the showcase store for Steinway pianos located in Manhattan. This was a unique privilege for the students and parents alike. The orchestra included several dozen strings players on violin, viola, and bass and a featured piano soloist, a young boy of unusual talent. Listening to the concert, if you closed your eyes, you would have no idea of the youthful age of the musicians. It was a magical evening. After the concert, the student musicians were given open access to the hall and its many beautiful pianos. Probably a dozen or so of the student musicians sat down at various spectacular Steinway pianos (remember, these were all strings students) and had their own mini concerts. That moment stuck with me. First at the multiple instrument talent, but more so that after performing a very challenging concert which had required months of preparation and endless hours of practice, these young musicians had such a passion and love of music that when the performance as over they wanted to play more!

The young musicians we enjoyed at Steinway Hall that evening were not special in any different way than every child around the world is special.

They were unique, however, in that they chose to participate in a very challenging program lead by a conductor who let them know from the beginning he had great expectations. In addition to their regular academic schedules, private music lessons, and school music programs, these kids (yes, with some parental prodding to be sure) devoted even more hours of their limited free time learning just how far their talent could take them. The result was a level of performance that amazed all who heard them perform, culminating that year in the rare and unique experience of performing at Steinway Hall. What they accomplished came directly from a choice to spend many hours developing talents and to the point of this book, saying "no" to the many possible and available distractions that most certainly would have diminished the level of performance they achieved.

Opportunity, resources, support--certainly all this plays a part. But the bottom line remains the same. This was a conscious choice to spend the many hours necessary to nurture and develop their musical abilities. I will tell you from close observation and my own very limited musical talent that there is no shortcut to a great performance... the hours must be spent in practice or it doesn't appear on stage.

Every life is different, every situation unique, but those who explore and nurture talents or skills, whatever they are, will uncover the wonderful, surprising and exciting array of abilities so vital in making life and culture alive and vibrant.

It takes all kinds of skills for a society to function, whether a person is an electrician or plumber, counselor or bringing beauty to the world like musicians or artists along with their teachers. There are great managers, crafts people, and motivators of people. Whatever the skill or talent, when a person finds that unique gift, it brings great satisfaction for both themselves and those who benefit from them and adds a strong and unique thread to the fabric of life.

Chapter 6: Owning Our Primary Task

Stop and think for a moment about your life so far and what will be the full length and breadth of your life in the end. What do you think of as your primary task? I know, that's a big question and it will change throughout life, to one degree or another, as the many moving parts of life change, but it does need to be asked. It's much easier, or at least more obvious, to break that down to a specific moment in time. The answer then becomes clear as well as much more unique to each person.

A student facing the SATs in a few weeks has a pretty clear primary task. New parents of an infant on the first day home from the hospital have a daunting, exciting and clear primary task. Someone recovering from a serious illness or managing a major life challenge has their own very personal primary task. The firefighters arriving on the scene of a house fire have an urgent, dangerous and critically important primary task.

Take a few more steps back and that primary task starts to get a bit more blurry. What about after the tests are done, graduation is over and you've started that first job? What about after the kids are grown and on their own? What about after the healing is done? What about after retirement from the fire department? What would we want to see as we gaze back on 70, 80 or even 90 years lived? Our life doesn't have to have a grand, world changing impact...it can be very simple, but certainly there will be a path that does come into focus. I have a lot of sympathy for the high school grads or those in the college search or even in the middle of college years and still not quite sure what they want to study and do with their life.

My youngest daughter explored a variety of expressions of the arts during her primary school years, including dance, music, and fine art. As the high school years moved along she had more focus on fine art, particularly in sculpture, and earned top awards in various art competitions even at regional levels which seemed to lead to a college choice focusing on fine arts. And while she did very well in her first year, there was still something missing. She eventually found architecture, another very exciting expression of artistic creativity, and is now pursuing that with great energy and enthusiasm. She has found her primary task as a student.

And what can happen when a primary task comes into sharp focus later in life?   If you are a baseball fan, you may remember the very tragic 180-degree turn in the baseball career of Daryl Strawberry, who played for both the Yankees and Mets. I had the pleasure of hearing Mr. Strawberry give a talk at a New Jersey high school in 2015. His talk was not about baseball per se. In fact, he started the talk asking the audience where the Met fans were (followed by some applause) then where the Yankee fans were (followed by some applause) then said very clearly that he was not going to talk about his glory years in baseball.

What he did share was a life story that very quickly changed the mood of anyone who thought they were going to hear about life as a pro ball player. He spoke about a very tragic life story, starting with painful early years with an abusive father, early use of drugs and alcohol, then in his high school years the discovery of incredible natural talent in baseball, an exciting rise as a very successful pro baseball player, followed by a fall from the highest peak of professional success to the lowest point he could imagine. As he went through his story, I would guess that many in the room were thinking about how anyone could throw away one of the most coveted positions in professional sport...playing at the top of your skills for the premier baseball team in the country with millions of fans cheering you and fortunes to be made. But all that slowly but steadily fell apart as drugs and alcohol took over his life. And that is what he was there to talk about, most specifically about the out of control growth of addiction to heroin across our country and likely in our own neighborhood.

Following this plunge to the lowest point, he had his own awakening and eventual recovery from addiction to become a minister and focus his energies on working with addicts through his rehab facilities which he funds with plans for more growth. What he was there to share was the horrible cost of drug addiction. He doesn't care about where these kids and adults come from. What he cares about is helping people claw their way back out of the dark pit of addiction and back into the light of a productive life.

Mr. Strawberry now has a crystal clear, passionate and powerful focus on his primary task.

He is fully committed to being one oasis for recovery- one light in the darkness of addiction. He knows what it's like to throw away God given gifts, whatever they may be, for what can only be called the ruthless and senseless distraction of drugs.

Mr. Strawberry has a unique life experience, notoriety, and financial means that all lead to his being able to do what he is doing. But at the same time, you have YOUR unique life path and situation that Mr. Strawberry does not.

You, at this moment, are a unique and special person capable of wonderful and most importantly, meaningful things, no matter what your age, life situation, or challenges. That meaningful thing does not have to be grand and far reaching. It may be to do less binge watching and pay more attention to your schoolwork and learn as much as you can while in your education years. It may be to pay more attention to your children and be present for their various activities and projects. It could be to reach out to a friend who needs a kind ear. Or to fully embrace the responsibilities of a job and perform that task the best way that you can.
Blessed Mother Theresa was quoted, "Not all of us can do great things. But we can do small things with great love." I think most would agree that there are far more small things done every day that if they were done with great love would make all the difference.

Chapter 7: The Why in the Road

Distraction is as old as time itself. The difference today is that with our very efficient, labor saving world with extremely easy access to entertainment and activities of all kinds and at all hours of day and night, it has become an all too easy drag on our lives. Consider the basic but pervasive problem of companies struggling to deal with employees spending an inordinate number of hours of the workday on Facebook and other social media sites. A recent study indicated that roughly 33 percent of companies actively block access to many social sites through company computers.

The following data comes from the site Biz30 article March 2015

Wasted Time in the Workplace – Infographic
Wasted time in the workplace is a massive problem. How big is exactly unclear, but from our research, the cost to business is in the millions (if not billions) in lost productivity every year.

The (information) below explains just how much time we waste at work, the ways we waste it, and how businesses are grappling with the issue. The results are surprising, if not alarming:

☐ 40% is the estimated productivity loss from non-work related internet surfing

☐ 54% of businesses now prohibit Facebook and Twitter access at work

☐ 14.2% (companies) actually blacklist Facebook access at work

☐ 70% of Internet pornography traffic occurs during the 9 to 5 work day

☐ 31.2% of workers believe it's appropriate to surf non-work related sites every day

☐ 21 hours a week, on average, are used by employees for non-work related web surfing

I think it would be fair to say that once any employee crossed the threshold of their place of employment, their primary task, at least for the day, should be very clear. Presumably employees believe they are being paid for every hour they are there at work and must logically assume they are doing some valuable task, providing a valuable service or otherwise are filling a job function important to the running of the organization. I seriously doubt the same employee who spends a few hours a day on company time updating Facebook would be happy to have paid a painter an hourly wage for a project on their house, stopping home to see the progress to find the project manager and the workers sitting around checking all the latest fantasy football stats. Might we apply the old wisdom of what's good for the goose is good for the gander?

But how often do we critically and carefully think "why am I doing this?" If a department manager came across an employee buried in Facebook while on the job, would the employee even struggle to explain whether work hours should be spent on social networking? The bigger question, as the distraction begins, is whether there is a moment when the question even occurs: "Why am I doing this right now? What is my primary task right now?" That is the critical moment...the Why in the road.

Unfortunately, on any particular day here in America, there is good chance for a person between 35 and 49 that roughly five hours was spent watching TV (Article March 5 2014, NY Daily News) and more TV and web time for those under age 35. For the news junkies, there is a benefit to keeping up with events in the world to stay informed. But at what point does a person pass from being informed and become simply obsessed or distracted? And especially if the news download is just to refuel the tank on all the reasons to hate some other point of view.

Some of us may need to decompress at the end of a stressful workday with some entertainment. But of what real value is the never-ending parade of "reality" shows where private persons can share their very personal day-to-day lives with millions of total strangers? Do I really need to know about a shopping trip for a pair of shoes with a price tag that could feed a village in Peru? Should I really care about the back biting, gossiping, and pettiness of strangers? When does curiosity about affluent spouses from around the country turn into hours and hours of what becomes an endless conga line of gossip?

What if we simply slowed down and asked ourselves these questions- Why am I doing this right now and why is this important? What would happen to ourselves, our families, our marriages, our communities, our country, and culture if each of us took a hard look at our own distractions, recognized them as distractions and treated each day, each hour like a gift — as a rare and precious gem, careful how it was cared for and spent?

Chapter 8: Life Isn't Easy, But It's Much Easier Than It Used to Be!

I know, many may be saying, "Hey, you don't know how hard it is out here!"

Life is not easy and never has been. In the story of Adam and Eve, it was basically a promise right after they lost their home in the perfection of Eden that from that point forward they would toil for their needs by the sweat of their brow. But relatively speaking, life is certainly much easier today then let's say even 250 years ago, which in the scale of human history is barely a blink of time. In the 1700s, just getting through a day was difficult. A typical frontier family in America was living on a farm taking care of virtually all their own needs. The day began before dawn and ended at dark, at least for the outdoor chores. Only a few mechanical aids were available and virtually all work was done with basic tools, working animals, and brute force. For example, if you didn't split wood, you had no heat and couldn't cook. And no heat on a long, dark bitter cold night in February on the open plains was quite literally deadly. If you didn't know how to keep the plow in good repair and the horse or mule healthy, you didn't plow, and if you didn't plow, you couldn't grow food.

Any number of diseases could kill you, and all kinds of bacteria and viruses could be in the food and water at any time. Oh, and for you germaphobes, no indoor plumbing. We watch the old westerns and see someone drinking out of every stream they came to, but the reality was any number of bacteria or a dead animal in the stream spoiled the water downstream for miles.

And while there were doctors in the cities, out on the plains the medical treatments were very limited, and they had only basic medicines for common illnesses. Even so, the harsh truth was that for most people medical help was far away.

The trading post or general store in the closest town provided, in most cases, various hardware items such as farm tools and basic raw ingredients for cooking such as flour and salt, but the farm provided the meat, eggs, and milk. Raising and caring for animals and tending crops was a non-stop responsibility (and by the way, if you know anyone working on a family farm, it still is non-stop!). It is not hyperbole to say just surviving in those days took effort. A family member not contributing, not making very good use of their time, had a direct impact on the well-being of the whole family.

One real life example of this lifestyle was featured on a TV mini-series from back in 2002 called Frontier House where the show producers had three families recreate those self-sufficient conditions mirroring life in 1883 Montana. The show started in early spring and each family had to build a cabin with rudimentary tools, grow and tend a garden, hunt for food and basically be totally self-sufficient. At the end of the show in late fall, the goal was to be prepared as though they would have to survive the harsh Montana winter.

There were various levels of success, and while some did well building reasonable shelter and preserving food, not ONE family had enough split wood for the winter. They all started much too late and none properly gauged how much wood they would need to keep warm all winter. In other words, they all would have been in very serious trouble in a few short months. Being prepared took MUCH more work than any of them appreciated. What they learned was that there was no time for distraction if they were to survive.

 The reality is that people throughout all human history had to figure this out in various ways based on their particular situation and conditions. Other than for the very wealthy, royalty and a few court jesters, leisure and rest for the general population was a luxury.

It has been this ongoing and very deliberate effort to live and thrive and improve that resulted in an algorithmic progression of invention, creativity, and productivity. For the generations born in the late 1800s living to see the mid to later 1900s, they saw the introduction of automobiles, expanding use of electricity and all the various electronic conveniences made possible because of access to electrical power. From that came refrigeration, which totally changed how food could be prepared and saved. The airplane went from a curiosity to a common mode of transportation. Prop planes turned to jets and soon the idea of space travel and landing on the moon went from a movie fantasy to multiple moon missions, followed by the development of the shuttle program and the establishment of the International Space Station. Generation after generation of hard-working people benefited from constant innovation, transforming more and more of our daily chores from being incredibly arduous to unthinkably easy.

Before we get too far down the road of feeling under-appreciated for the 10 hour day we put in, it's likely we woke up in a warm (or cool) house or apartment, enjoyed the convenience of indoor plumbing, turned a faucet to enjoy a hot shower, flipped a knob to make a pot of coffee, opened the frig for our breakfast, got to our job or classes in an air conditioned or heated bus, train, or car. Most people work in a heated or cooled building, have access to clean water, hot coffee and food throughout the day, have little or no chance of facing death or serious injury (the lousy chili dog you ate at lunch doesn't count). If we are feeling a bit ill, most have the option to stay home in a warm bed and if we don't feel much better by day two can make an appointment to see our doctor, get a prescription for an efficacious medication and be back to our routine once healed. So, on the whole, it's better than struggling through a rocky field with an old plow behind a stubborn mule on a cold spring day after a morning rain, soaked to the skin and shivering trying to get the field plowed before sundown so the seed can get in the ground, all the while keeping a wary eye out for the bear that is roaming the area #icoulddietoday. Upon reflection, most would agree that the slow line at your favorite coffee spot is a much preferred #firstworldproblem.

The incredible advances in productivity in the last few hundred years have resulted in the ability to get far more done by far fewer people with much less effort. As for planting and plowing, with today's available equipment, one farmer and a very small team can plow, plant and harvest what would require literally hundreds of work animals and people. From manufacturing techniques, to food production, to all areas of life, we are getting better and better at producing more with less effort which in turn allows us, in the main, to enjoy what would have been thought of just 250 years ago as unimaginable leisure. Leisure in and of itself can be a very good and necessary break in our routine. But what may have once been thought of as a privilege or fruits of hard work and enjoyed with deliberate intent has become an expectation, not only for weekends and the few weeks of vacation each year, but also in smaller ways throughout each day in many and various empty and useless distractions common in so many lives. (Consider the work hour distraction stats from the Time Doctor Blog from Chapter 7

For the ancient Greeks, leisure provided to the wealthy spawned some of the world's greatest philosophical thinking from minds like Plato, Socrates, and Aristotle. Aristotle's approach focused on understanding the "why" of all things. In our own recent American historical figures, John Adams, one of our founding fathers, wished that his family could enjoy happiness, but his definition did not mean idleness; it meant the happiness of learning and growing in knowledge of the world, arts, sciences, and more. Martin Luther King wanted to move the country beyond deeply ingrained prejudices, look past skin color and deeper into the value of each person.

For many of the great thinkers in history, the "why" was very clear. The primary task was to grow, develop, and contribute. Now before anyone starts pointing out the faults, missteps, and errors of various leaders and thinkers, I would caution anyone to assume any mortal human being represents perfection.

What many in history have done is try to pursue an ideal, some worthy and noble and others not. Those noble ideals are easily identified, but we can't be distracted by the ideal not being achieved by any particular individual. Do we dismiss all the athletes in the Olympic track events who cross the line after first place as failures? They didn't reach their ideal, after all. They didn't win. Well, of course not. We admire their goal, their focused effort, their dedication to the ideal... of striving to be their best. The same applies to many areas of life. If the ideal being pursued is noble, good, true, and valuable, then it is worth cheering, supporting, and nurturing all those working towards its achievement.

Chapter 9: Learning to Say NO

A number of years ago I was listening to a radio program featuring a very interesting study where the author set out to understand what made a specific group of creative people so successful...what traits, habits, etc. contributed to their success. Well, the answer came in an unexpected way. Of the hundreds of requests for interviews, roughly one third simply didn't reply, one third had some other individual or staff member answer for them indicating they had no interest in participating, and the final third was a mix of responses. Among the written responses, the most common refrain was that being truly productive required saying NO to useless, unproductive tasks or distractions that took them away from their work. The ability and willingness to say NO was the most common answer...and these particularly successful creative people said the interview was not a productive use of their time. Ouch!

Now that is a very interesting thing to ponder. Take a moment to think about this response. What do we say yes to that, if we're honest with ourselves, is nothing more than distraction? Do we think deliberately and seriously about our core responsibilities and roles as important enough that we should make that choice to say no to activities which get in the way?

You have probably heard the often-repeated adage "If you want to get something done, give it to a busy person," and there is some truth in that. But taking this from the vantage point of the busy person, is there a chance that, to some degree, taking on too much has more to do with feeling important than it has to do with truly having the time for yet another project? I'm not talking about urgent matters or emergency situations or the reality of parents juggling all the needs of their family and running a house. I'm talking about the people who seem to be involved in every activity around town or every project at the office. While the push for being hyper productive has led to learning to multitask, more and more studies are proving that multi-tasking (doing multiple things at the same time) is far from productive.

From Inc. on line, May 11, 2017

"We sacrifice our power of full presence when we're multitasking, and we do so for a perceived benefit of improved productivity that simply doesn't exist. Research indicates that multitaskers are actually less likely to be productive, yet they feel more emotionally satisfied with their work, thus creating an illusion of productivity. This bears repeating. Forget for a moment that multitasking can be incredibly rude, we're not actually accomplishing what we think we are--we've been fooling ourselves."

The article does go on to point out that "task shifting," switching quickly from one task to the other, may seem better but even that ends up with poor actual results. The article goes on to say, "A Stanford study confirmed this by showing that those who multitask are indeed worse performers, and struggle because they can't filter out irrelevant information, slowing down completion of the cognitive task at hand."

Back to the start of this book and the point that at any particular stage of life or point in time we very likely have a primary task which should rise above all other activities or responsibilities. The above statement "...can't filter out the irrelevant information..." also touches on one of the definitions of distraction presented at the start of the book.

"An interruption to attention or anything that draws attention away from a primary task."

It's as simple as paying attention to what is in front of us. At the soccer field, we may get a lot more out of the afternoon when we turn the ringer off the phone and watch the game. On the job, we may improve our performance if we turn off the social media and focus on completing the project. It's not complicated, but it takes discipline and focus.

Chapter 10: Discovering and nurturing our unique gifts and talents

In our quiet moments, we do understand why we are worth the effort to improve ourselves and see the irreplaceable part we play in other people's lives. We know we are unique and important to the people entrusted to us. We probably want to be productive and use the gifts we have been given exploring the fullest possible expression of ourselves and supporting those around us who need us to help them along on the journey of life.

We don't have to look far to discover talents and gifts. Some talented people are easily identified. If you have ever been close by watching a house be built, it's really quite amazing to see all the various skills needed to go from an empty piece of land, to a hole in the ground, to foundation, to frame, and eventually to a home. Most of us have had the experience of getting some odd car problem diagnosed and fixed by a talented mechanic. Or what about the doctor that sees something no one else did?

But what about the quieter and more personal gifts? Have you ever had the wonderful blessing of a friend who just makes you feel safe, feel important... someone who is great at listening and can help you work through life's challenges? Well, that's a gift. Have you ever worked with someone who has a knack for cutting right through a problem to see the solution? That's a talent.

Have you ever seen a young parent patiently teaching a child to ride a bike? That is a gift. Do you know anyone who seems to be able to be kind to even the most irritable person? That's a wonderful gift. What about people who get through every day facing an almost constant barrage of challenges and difficulties, whether they be financial, emotional or physical, and do it with calm determination? That is a gift.

We see it all the time, we even may do it all the time. Love, charity, patience, kindness, understanding, fortitude...these are all gifts that impact people every day, every hour, every minute of life and ultimately are far more important to our lives than running the fastest mile or achieving significant financial success.

However, life events can get in the way. It is very easy to be terribly discouraged. For some, a life situation can be alarmingly difficult and make simply getting through the day a daunting task. For others who may have professional success, the various pressures and distractions of managing a career or company can turn those advantages into a constant distraction from family and friends. For the poor, the constant stress of worry about meeting basic daily material needs and how that impacts their family can be overwhelming.

This next section is particularly important, and I would ask you to please pause for a few minutes to let it sink in.

First, a quote. I won't say the source right now so there are no prejudices either way. A very close friend gave me this quote when I was going through a particularly difficult time and I believe that this has value for every person to consider.

"Consult not your fears but your hopes and your dreams. Think not of your frustrations, but about your unfulfilled potential. Concern yourself not with what you tried and failed in, but with what is still possible for you to do."

There are so many ways a person can pursue and nurture gifts and talents. But I don't follow the often-repeated promise to kids that you can be anything you want. At 5'8" and 180 pounds (OK, fine, at 5' 7.5" and 190 pounds), I cannot play center for the Miami Heat nor linebacker for the NY Giants. But if I love sports, I CAN learn all about sports management, get into broadcasting and become a sports commentator, a sports physician or trainer. I can't be ANYTHING I want, but I absolutely can nurture the gifts I have in pursuit of a passion for the MANY things I can be. Yes, there are gifted athletes, doctors, inventors and others who end up at the very top of their field and you may be one of those. Start with your natural talents and gifts and then try to figure out what gets your blood pumping, ignore artificial barriers and the naysayers and then find a place where talents, gifts, and interests intersect.

It may also be that the thing that gets our blood pumping is in addition to a profession. Try this experiment the next time you're at an event with live musicians. At a break or after the show, ask a few of the musicians if playing music is what they do for a living. You may be surprised to find out that a high percentage have daytime jobs to pay the bills, but their unique gift for music is expressed as a second job or just occasional gig. So a passion that contributes to the rich fabric of life may find its way into our lives, not as a profession, but as a hobby.

I think of my grandparents on my mother's side as a great example. My grandfather was a very talented musician and played professional banjo in a concert band in his younger years. My grandmother had a very difficult life but did learn to play piano. When the Depression came, my grandfather had to give up music and worked in a gas station/car repair shop for many years, while my grandmother did various jobs to help pay the bills and raise a family. In their later years, they moved to a retirement community and immediately formed a band, with my grandmother playing piano and my grandfather doing music transposing for the various instruments. It was hard to catch them at home. They were often practicing or playing "gigs," mostly at hospitals, retirement homes, and the like. And they kept doing this into their 90s! Their gifts for music were a blessing to thousands of people in their final years.

Our ability to contribute and make a difference is not contingent on material wealth or social standing. The list is endless as to what we can accomplish should we have a mind to explore and develop as a human person IF we clearly understand that we are each a unique thread in the fabric of life and have been given gifts and talents for a reason. What a difference it makes if we accept and embrace the responsibility to ourselves to grow as a person and to use our gifts to support, nurture and treasure the people put into your life.

Every person reading this book is fully capable of contributing to one degree or another. We are not all Edisons, Sullivans, Mozarts, Gates, or Ghandis, nor should we be. Electricity is only valuable if people build infrastructures to safely distribute it. My son worked in production at a beautiful outdoor music venue in the rolling hills of Sullivan County NY, called Bethel Woods Performing Arts Center, built on the site of Woodstock. (Yes, THAT Woodstock) It was amazing to learn about all the work he and the production team did in putting on a concert. Long before the crowd arrives, he and the team have been on the job for many hours in preparation of the grounds, staging, sound work, food prep, and product vendors...the list is endless to ensure a great patron experience. Then, when the show is over, they are on the job for another few hours managing everything from the parking staff getting people moving out efficiently and quickly, putting equipment away, coiling up all those sound cords and generally cleaning up the venue and preparing for the next day's show. Thanks to all that work and preparation, a concert is all the more enjoyable. So it is in our daily lives. It is this vast mix of jobs and tasks and the people who do the work with focus and attention to detail that make communities and cultures work.

The sad truth is that far too many of us have very stubborn, very persistent distractions filling our lives and hearts, and before we can make that choice to live the life we are capable of, we must take the time to look very hard at what is in our way. How many of these distractions we choose to push aside can start right now?

Chapter 11: What It Is and What It Isn't

It's time to dig into the real heart of the issue of identifying distractions and separating out what is just part of normal and expected interruption and what is pulling us away from our potential as people and responsibilities as an individual. Because at the heart of it the issue is what is extra and avoidable that is getting in the way of reaching our potential.

It's also important to keep remembering that each person is in a unique situation and what may seem like distraction to one person is actually an integral and unavoidable part of another's. We can't all choose our responsibilities and we also don't all have the ability to contribute the same way. A 16-year old high school student has a very different life then a 20-something in a first job. The parent of infants and young kids has very different responsibilities than a retired person. Those who are struggling with illness or injury have a greater duty to self-healing than to helping others. So, within each of our lives and situations, understand that the goal is to separate out what are appropriate and necessary activities and the normal day-to-day stimulations of life vs. those that get in the way of our lives, our responsibilities, our families.

When we start to look at our lives and what fills it with new eyes, with a new sense of purpose, it will become more and more clear where the changes need to happen. Remember that habits are similar to addictions.

Some will be harder to change than others. There is an old story about a teacher explaining bad habits to a student. The teacher takes the student out into a field and asks the student to pull up a small weed, which they do easily. Then they proceed on to a larger plant, which takes more effort. Next is a small bush which eventually is pulled free. Then they move on to a tree sapling. After much effort and sweat, the student only begins to barely shift the deep roots. The teacher then explains to the student that habits are the same. The older and larger the plant and deeper the roots, the harder it is to remove.

Getting back to distractions, at this very moment, can you honestly say that 100 percent of your focus is on the words in front of you? As thought provoking as I hope this subject is, I would say probably not, at least not yet. But complete focus on any task is not easy. We want to focus but so many stimulations get in the way. Most of us genuinely want to be able to focus attention, be productive, live a good life exploring gifts and talents as well as care for the people around us and to reach our final years knowing we used our time well and that we made a difference. I do believe this. However, even the relatively innocent forms of entertainment and activities available in our modern world have an insidious way of pulling our attention away from what ought to be done.

When it comes to basic concentration, like reading this book right now, distraction starts with small things and it's hard to avoid. Your brain is picking up sounds, smells, glimpses of things happening around you, something in the room you see or your mobile phone buzzing with a new message. Maybe you're hungry or thirsty or have a song stuck in your head or a piece of chicken stuck in your teeth. There may be an event still crowding your thoughts like a hyperactive puppy tugging at your mind's shirtsleeve. To a certain degree this is good, because your senses are doing their job. In fact, it's estimated that the human brain processes about 40 billion bits of information per second. It must be able to do that for a reason.

On the other hand, there is the almost contrary fact that we don't consciously pay attention to much at all. Carl Jung, the famous Swiss psychologist, said that more than 90 percent of our lives are lived unconsciously. And if we're honest with ourselves, we would admit that most of our daily lives are lived as a routine. Do we really think about our breakfast, showering, brushing teeth? What about the bus ride or drive to school or work? Even the simple routine of everyday responsibilities can flow past us with little attention. For anyone who drives often and on a repeated route, have you ever found yourself at a light or your destination and you literally cannot remember the last portion of the drive? And to some degree this is an emotional self-defense. We need to do some things without intense focus to avoid sensory overload (Okay, maybe the driving needs to be done with focused attention).

It's necessary for the parent getting the kids ready for school in the morning to be able to listen to their sixth grader explain the after-school game they are attending and that they need a ride home, while the two other siblings are arguing about whose turn it is to walk the dog, asking the parent for the tie-breaking vote, while at the same time making lunches, putting the breakfast dishes in the dishwasher, and checking backpacks to make sure all is ready to go. At work it's a valuable skill for a small business owner to juggle a dozen issues in their head managing people, inventory, billing, payroll, the marketing plan, maintenance, and other things to keep the business alive and profitable. It's job security for an administrator to keep multiple projects and requests moving along and completed on time. What I am talking about is something different.

There is a delicate balance between how we make it through the day sifting through what is important and what is not, what we easily manage as simple routine or a break in that routine, what catches our attention and what we ignore and the things we choose to bring into our life that take us away from far more vital and immediate priorities.

When we really pay attention and think about focused attention, not just to a task, but to life, we see young and old alike distracted by activities and interests that become self-absorbing and at times self-destructive. There are only so many waking hours in the day, days a year, and years in our lives. Life isn't a video game where we can just push a button to restart from the beginning as often as we want. While I absolutely believe we all deserve fresh starts, unlike the game, our restart picks up where we left off, not at the beginning. Put in more stark terms, we don't have some other life we will get to start from the beginning that affords us the luxury to waste very much of this one. If we are to take care of ourselves, our families, and our communities, we must take a hard look at just what we're doing with our time.

Chapter 12: Our Many and Complex Inner Turmoils

Emotional distractions can be particularly insidious. They not only interrupt basic responsibilities, but more importantly often don't resolve any issue or serve a positive purpose. It can be a thought, an event, or anticipation of something in the future. Maybe it's an argument with a co-worker that becomes an all-consuming thought bouncing around and around someone's mind, and as 5:00 comes there is the realization that the day was consumed by it. Thinking through some major event can be beneficial if it results in some resolution, but if not, it only takes away from focusing on the day at hand and the responsibilities of the job. What if that person were the doctor diagnosing an illness or a nurse managing a complex mix of medications for a patient, or a hospital administrator keeping patient records accurate and up to date? How confident would you be that the proper full attention was on their job when a life hangs in the balance? You may be thinking, this is a bit of an overreaction.

"Washington, D.C., October 23, 2013 – New research estimates up to 440,000 Americans are dying annually from preventable hospital errors. This puts medical errors as the third leading cause of death in the United States, underscoring the need for patients to protect themselves and their families from harm, and for hospitals to make patient safety a priority."
[www.hospitalsafetygrade.org]

Fair enough that we don't know the reason for all these errors, such as short staffing, long hours and high stress, but assuming that the vast majority of medical professionals are very smart and capable people, is it reasonable to assume that distraction and lack of focus has played a part?

Emotional distraction can also come from the very real pressures of life. Financial issues, family strains, difficult friendships, and overwhelming events can weigh heavily on a person's mind every day, every hour, every moment. We know logically that worry doesn't ultimately change situations. Stress is one of the more difficult distractions to manage for anyone and in fact, based on many recent studies, stress about the many and very real challenges in life does significant physical and emotional damage. A 2015 article by the Mayo Clinic staff on stress pointed out that symptoms of stress can impact the body, thoughts, feelings, and behavior. Symptoms included headache, muscle tension or pain and fatigue. Impacts included angry outbursts, drug or alcohol abuse and social withdrawal. So there is more than enough reason to deal with stress at the very first signs.

A recent survey indicated that roughly one third of adult Americans are taking some form of anti-depressant. There is clearly a growing problem of people unable to cope with the stresses of life requiring drugs to compensate. This level of stress can be anything from an inconvenience to an all-consuming focus. Certainly, there are cases of true diagnosed need, but one third of the adult population?

Among those adults there must be spouses, parents, teachers, bosses, neighbors who have people counting on them. What are we letting seep into our lives that creates this unmanageable stress resulting in such widespread need?

The same could be said of jealousy, rage, and bitterness. If you've lived long enough, you have met people with simmering anger or a bitterness that invades their whole life. It would not be surprising to look back enough years in that person's life and find a happy, content person before bitterness took root. In many ways, emotional distractions are not all that less distracting to a better life than the drug to the addict. It is very likely those around them would see an obvious difference between the eager, lively young adult and the older, bitter person they have become. Bitterness can't help but distract from being open to people and relationships around us and keep us from living a more open and loving life.

Not many years ago from the writing of this book there was a horrible incident in an Amish community in Lancaster, Pennsylvania where 10 young girls were shot and killed in a one-room schoolhouse. To many people's shock and surprise, this community made a conscious decision to forgive the attacker. This was NOT an approval of what happened. It was a choice to let go of the distraction that bitterness and hatred would do to them as a community. It was a choice to pray for their community as well as the attacker and not let anger distract them from the main principles, values, and purpose of their Amish community and move forward with life.

The story got national attention, not so much because people admired this response, but shock of "how could they?" Might the public response actually have come from guilt in the hearts of so many people as their conscience pricked them just a bit? The offending thought being, "And I can't even forgive that foolish thing said at a family gathering 16 years ago." I think it could be the people who were so shocked just couldn't understand that kind of forgiveness. Could it be that many do indeed think of forgiveness as approval? Forgiveness, in part, is a decision to not let an event or incident be carried forward like some black sack filled with an ugly object emitting a foul stench. The Amish community knew if they didn't let go right away, any lingering bitterness would do nothing to the killer, nor bring their children back, but it most definitely would eat away at their own hearts every day. The old saying is quite true...bitterness is like drinking poison thinking it will kill your enemy.

Clearly this is an example difficult to imagine in our own lives, and we don't know to what degree each member of that Amish community ultimately succeeded in moving forward, but the reality was that forgiveness was their firm purpose and after all, that's where so many tough things in life begin...choosing a direction and starting the journey with firm resolve.

There are some situations which are very personal, very

hurtful, and very difficult to even comprehend. There are those very difficult choices when hurtful people who do not have our best interest at heart should be avoided or even eliminated from our daily lives. The point is, we have a choice to either hang on to anger and bitterness or, as difficult as it may be, to at least choose to try and forgive, let go, and move forward. It would seem to be fairly safe to say that bitterness will distract us for sure. Does forgiveness at least provide the chance for more loving relationships and a happier life?

A much less intense, but interesting example of how our emotional distractions and sense of revenge affect our decisions was presented on an episode of a TV show called Brain Games. If you have not seen the show, the premise is that our brains take in and process information, stimulation, and distraction in very interesting ways. The show explores just how our brains work and observation skills and behavior are affected in various situations.

On one episode they set up a coffee shop where a service person, a personable young woman, would deliberately give people paying with cash excess change, in this case an extra $20. For the first portion of the show, she was extremely pleasant and helpful, provided prompt service and was generally wonderful to work with. In virtually every case where she gave the extra $20 in change, the patrons let her know and returned it. (I guess there were one or two few cash strapped folks.)

The same situation was run again, but this time the young

woman was distracted, rude, unpleasant, and often on her cell phone, almost ignoring the customer at the counter. Again, she provided excess change of $20, but this time only one person out of roughly eight gave back the $20.

When the patrons were interviewed afterward, having been told about the experiment, those who did not return the $20 to the "distracted" barista explained that they thought the girl deserved to get in trouble for giving back wrong change, thinking it would teach her to be more pleasant, more attentive, and less distracted.
It was interesting that customers thought distraction from doing a proper job was not only unpleasant but deserved a bit of financial pain as well. When we put on a sour face out of anger or bitterness and become immersed in our own problems ignoring the people right in front of us who have nothing to do with whatever is eating at us, we are unconsciously giving permission to be treated poorly. Conversely, we can spread a smile and pay attention and will be inviting a bit of patience and kindness.

Chapter 13: The Technology and Social Media Conundrum

Advances in technology have touched almost every aspect of daily life. It is almost too obvious to mention. Just on the subject of information gathering and use, it has brought with it incredibly expanded access as well as the ability to analyze and use data in ways unthinkable not 50 years ago. The sciences have become more and more accessible and more impactful as well. Our local school district participated in a program called Science Olympiad. The main thrust was to have students compete in various events based on knowledge and application of scientific principles in a variety of science related challenges. My son enjoyed participating with a good friend and other classmates in several competitions, such as building and flying a model helicopter made of only balsa wood and using a rubber band for power, building and using a catapult device to perform within very specific requirements, learning and testing knowledge of birds, building and running robots...the list was endless. Competitions revolved around learning or taking scientific principles and putting them to actual use, providing a competitive and fun platform for kids who loved learning and spark an interest in the sciences as a career. So, there are wonderful, beneficial, and amazing places where technology and science can enrich our lives.

The incredible expansion of the volume and speed of data transmission has provided a technical environment for services which can handle and share huge amounts of data. As this expansion of technology grew, what was first only the tool of business and science, purely social and leisure applications suddenly became cost effective and practical. From that came the advent of social media, which has had some interesting and fascinating benefits. Various social media platforms for getting and keeping in touch have brought many people together who would otherwise either never see each other or never get to know each other. I think of a friend here in the U.S. who had a brother who moved to New Zealand. While a half a world away, they were able to use various social media and video to talk to each other, keeping them up to date and connected. This same technology allows parents to not just talk to, but see their kids who are away at college. (Don't worry, they'll still be back with huge sacks of laundry!)

Communication technology and the web can allow long-lost friends to reconnect or arrange reunions. I was able to help organize my own 30-year high school reunion, connecting with almost 217 out of a class of almost 260, thanks in large part to social media. This is complimented with the ubiquitous nature of personal cellular devices, making it possible to remain "connected" virtually every waking hour of every day, and unfortunately even interrupting what should be the non-waking hours as well.

With all the benefits, there is another growing darker side to this hyper connected world. It's what could be called the new relationship day traders.

For those who may not be familiar with the term "day trader," these are people who invest in the stock market for very short time periods, often within the same trading day, and even within the same hour at times. The nature of the day trader is that they must keep a very careful watch on their investments and trades throughout the day to not miss any unanticipated price movements up or down.

With that said, observe the crowd in a typical casual serve restaurant or cafe and see how many people sitting together at a table are spending most of their time texting or messaging someone not at the table. One would assume that they came out to sit together and catch up or, perish the thought, relax and unplug. But for many people, they can't get away from needing to stay connected to some other events, notes, snaps, checking "likes," texts for even just a few minutes to enjoy the company of the person sitting with them. And they seem to be okay with the arrangement. But consider for a moment how texting has evolved to include all kinds of graphic elements to express emotions etc. that are difficult to capture in words. What about Snapchat and other quick video access tools? It implies we want to express more exactly how we are feeling. So back to the café...the very best "expression" possible is with the live person sitting with you. This is the chance to have deep, important, expressive discussions and the people who are sitting at the table together are the best opportunity, yes? Well, looking at a typical gathering at a café or coffee shop, it's a very far cry from the ageless tradition of the French street café' where Parisians would enjoy a bit of sun, some lively discussion and, most importantly, friendship.

On the far edge of the negative effects is an explosion of narcissism. A June 30, 2017 Article from the website The Journal is titled "Study shows sharp increase in Narcissism among teens who use Facebook," the first few paragraphs should give us pause just how much time we substitute real live human relationships with virtual ones.

> *"Recent studies have indicated a sharp increase in narcissism, self-promotional and anti-social behavior among teens who use social media frequently, especially Facebook and Instagram.*
> *One study by Christopher Carpenter in the journal Personality and Individual Differences found that rates of narcissism and self-promotional behavior increased with the increased use of Facebook.*
> *In the United States, diagnoses of narcissistic personality disorder (NPD) have risen sharply over the past 10 years, according to the Guardian. The rate is comparable to the rise in the rate of obesity, the Guardian reports..."*

And before we panic, this is not to dismiss Facebook or any other social networking platform out of hand. They can be used with great benefit, keeping people in touch and making connections that would otherwise be difficult or not possible. It's a matter of proportion and balance and seeing that nothing replaces real person to person relationships.

But what makes us so uneasy about quiet, simple face-to-face conversation? It was Blaise Pascal, the French philosopher born back in 1623, who said that "all of humanity's problems stem from (people's) inability to sit quietly in a room for one hour alone." This implies that we need to be happy with who we are before we can be at ease with others.

Chapter 14: Tech Savvy or Tech Slaves?

My career started in marketing. In my early years we used all paper communications. Reports were created with drawn charts and lots of number crunching. Companies told their stories with brochures, letters, space advertising, and endless in-person meetings and events. The advent of PCs and word processors, fax machines, and other technologies gave us time and money savings to get much more done, faster and with fewer people. With these and the newer communication tools, companies can now email, tweet, blog, and generally spread news almost instantly. You would think all these labor-saving solutions would afford us more time, but it does not. It affords us getting even more done each day with greater and greater pressure to work faster and more efficiently.

We have gone from technologies that made work more efficient to technologies that demand our attention every day all day. You can make the case that these tools and leveraging their speed and productivity is necessary to be competitive. And there is truth in that, but where does it stop and at what price? The way companies and technologies get more and more speed out of communication lines is quite fascinating. Just to focus on fiber optics, since light travels at a set speed, it's not possible to increase the speed of the transmission. The information travels in "packets" along the lines, so the speed is realized by filling in ever smaller spaces in between the packets of data. As a life analogy, are we willing to fill up each moment, each space filled with productivity? Is that our goal? Going back to the survey finding roughly 70 percent of American workers are disengaged at work, is disengagement a response to productivity overload or are there much more complex issues going on?

This might be a good moment to think back to the popular Harry Chapin song "Cats in the Cradle" and the distracted father. For anyone not familiar with the song, the theme surrounds a son and the always too busy father promising to "get together sometime" and always breaking the promise. The son says to himself that he will grow up to be just like his father and in the end, when his father finally realizes he wants to spend time with his son, the son is too busy. Will the cycle continue for the son into the next generation, we wonder?

But back to the general population, outside of business, some may believe that we are just seeing the growth of a very tech savvy generation. If you were to ask where the general American public ranked with proficiency and effective use of technology, most would say we would rank at or close to the top. After all, technology is everywhere in the U.S. Who doesn't have a smart phone and several other devices with hundreds of applications? We're a connected society, right? You may want to sit down for this.

The following is from the Fortune magazine website article by Anne Fisher, March 10, 2015 titled "American Millennial's are among the worlds' least skilled."

Here are a few excerpts that may surprise you.

"We hear about the superior tech savvy of people born after 1980 so often that we tend to assume it must be true. But is it?

Researchers at Princeton-based Educational Testing Service (ETS) expected it to be when they administered a test called the Program for the International Assessment of Adult Competencies (PIAAC). Sponsored by the OECD, the test was designed to measure the job skills of adults, aged 16 to 65, in 23 countries.

When the results were analyzed by age group and nationality, ETS got a shock. It turns out, says a new report, that Millennials in the U.S. fall short when it comes to the skills employers want most: literacy (including the ability to follow simple instructions), practical math, and — hold on to your hat — a category called "problem-solving in technology-rich environments."

Not only do Gen Y Americans lag far behind their overseas peers by every measure, but they even score lower than other age groups of Americans.

Take literacy, for instance. American Millennials scored lower than their counterparts in every country that participated except Spain and Italy. (Japan is No. 1.) In numeracy, meaning the ability to apply basic math to everyday situations, Gen Yers in the U.S. ranked dead last."

Okay, but what about making smart use of technology, where Millennials are said to shine? Again, America scored at the bottom of the heap, in a four-way tie for last place with the Slovak Republic, Ireland, and Poland.

Even the best-educated Millennials stateside couldn't compete with their counterparts in Japan, Finland, South Korea, Belgium, Sweden, or elsewhere. With a master's degree, for example, Americans scored higher in numeracy than peers in just three countries: Ireland, Poland, and Spain. Altogether, the top U.S. Gen Yers, in the 90th percentile, "scored lower than their counterparts in 15 countries," the report notes, "and only scored higher than their peers in Spain."

Yes we HAVE a lot of technology, but what the average American is DOING with technology is unfortunately a lot of very basic functions and endless entertainment. Just watch any TV ad about the speed of a particular telecom service platform. What do they show to prove the "value" of their service? Mostly they show how easily a movie or video game loads and runs or how the whole family can be buried in their own devices at the same time avoiding all that annoying family interaction. On the whole we are not developing, learning, advancing, or expanding our understanding of our world. We are gaming, texting, tweeting, YouTubing and generally doing what takes about a sixth-grade education to master. The analogy would be that a group of string students were given priceless Stradivarius violins with much fanfare. They would be presented as having the very finest violins known to exist.

Well, if they only learned to play Twinkle, Twinkle Little Star, isn't it a horrible waste of instruments?

Consider the ideal from the 1400s and what was known at the time as the Renaissance man, also called Universal Man, an ideal that developed in Renaissance Italy from the idea that "a (person) can do all things if (they) will." The idea came from Renaissance Humanism, which considered man (humankind) limitless in the capacity for development, and that we should try to embrace all knowledge and develop capacities as fully as possible. The following excerpt is from the Encyclopedia Brittanica: Thus the gifted men of the Renaissance sought to develop skills in all areas of knowledge, in physical development, in social accomplishments, and in the arts. The ideal was most brilliantly exemplified in Alberti—who was an accomplished architect, painter, classicist, poet, scientist, and mathematician and who also boasted of his skill as a horseman and in physical feats—and in Leonardo da Vinci (1452–1519), whose gifts were manifest in the fields of art, science, music, invention, and writing.

This ideal was unique since very few people had the combination of access to books and the time to freedom to spend learning. Keep in mind, the printing press was invented in 1440 by Johannes Gutenberg, but until then books were still individually hand written and illustrated, rare and very expensive. It was a unique opportunity to read and study. At that time life was difficult at best and most people were involved in physical labor of some sort.

Taking time to read and study meant less time farming, milling, blacksmithing...you get the idea. A good number of the great artists of that time were supported by what was known as a "commissioner" to pursue their art. Today, virtually the entire population has access to almost any bit of knowledge we can imagine, so the remaining piece is the freedom of at least some leisure time to pursue and use at least some of that knowledge.

While we have access to the contents of the Library of Congress in our pockets, our most exciting achievement in free time for many is reaching the next level of Candy Crush. Playing video games on occasion for entertainment is not the problem. Go back to college freshmen increasingly needing remedial instruction in English and Math, all while having the knowledge of the ages on this compact device in their pocket.

Chapter 15: Using our Time

Sign over a Tavern Bar "Free Beer Tomorrow"

It takes a second, but then we get the joke...it's never tomorrow. It's always today.

We can only live in the present. This seems simple enough, but consider this very carefully. We can talk about the past or the future, consider what could have been or what might be. And there is value is learning from the past and planning for the future...but we can only live in the present. Imagine trying to drive a car, only able to see out the rear-view mirror or somewhere far down the road you haven't arrived at yet? You'd be in big trouble very quickly if you didn't pay attention to exactly where the vehicle was at every moment. To avoid danger, you must be most focused on where you are. Is this so much different than life?

Each moment, each "now" is all we can live in. Procrastination is the ability to convince ourselves that whatever it is we are pondering does not have to be done now. The reasoning is there are many other future opportunities to accomplish that unsavory task, but are there? There is a deep truth in the saying "there is no time like the present." This moment is unique, just like the next moment will be unique, but possibly unique in a way that is not to our benefit. The moment to take the kids to the park at 10:00 while the sun was shining gets put off till after the big game on TV and then a few hours later the rain has started.

The opportunity to sit down to talk with a loved one about a very important decision is put off until after finishing Level 5 in a video game and then a few hours later the mood has changed and the next "now" makes what needed to get done or said more difficult, or not possible at all. Time only moves forward, and the infinitely complex intertwining of lives and events can't help but intersect with and affect our plans.

The present moment is important in many ways. Precious moments that will be a memory for a lifetime can come from any situation or activity. While walking along a residential street on a warm summer afternoon, I came across an adorable scene of two little girls, apparently sisters, I would guess about 5 and 8 years old. The older sister was trying to teach the younger one how to do the "wheelbarrow," holding up her sister's legs while she walked on her hands. Well, the younger girl wasn't quite getting it, but the two of them were laughing and giggling trying to coordinate their efforts. Sitting on the porch just a few feet away was the mom, buried in a cell phone, not even paying attention to this wonderful little moment. As a parent, I looked at this moment and saw it as a wonderful slice of life, a funny story to tell for years to come and a memory to warm a parent's heart. Was that call or text more important at that moment? Possibly, but it was still a memory lost for the mom.

Talk to a person in their later years about time. There is a reason that the seniors among us almost without fail will say the same things about time. Don't waste it. It goes by faster than you realize. Pick one of the countless quaint comments about time and they all revolve around the common theme that it moves far more quickly than we realize and woe to the one who wastes it. For those readers familiar with the band Pink Floyd, a song "Time" from the Dark Side of the Moon album makes this point quite well.

> "...and then one day you'll find
> ten years have got behind you
> No one told you when to run,
> you missed the starting gun."

So we should slow down long enough to accept that time only moves forward and faster than we realize, so what we do with it, how we spend it, who we spend it in all makes a tremendous difference to ourselves, our families, and our communities.

Whether we are aware of it or not, the life of any community absolutely relies on people giving of themselves, volunteers who roll up their sleeves to do things that need to get done not for money, but for the good of the community. If you read about a small-town fire, who responds? That would be volunteers. Ever see the local churches doing food drives? What about all those sport coaches for the school? Yup, more volunteers. School boards, soup kitchens, food banks, after school programs?

More volunteers. Take out volunteers and many basic services and needs collapse. People giving of their time are the life blood of communities.

If you are, have been, or know parents of young children, then you already know the answer about sacrificing time. From losing sleep being up in the middle of the night with sick children, to all the various running around to get the kids to and from school to this or that activity, it all takes a conscious choice to prioritize children within the limited free hours each day. The same is true in any relationship. Time is spent and sacrifices are made to keep the relationship alive and growing.

With just a little bit of self-awareness, I believe we will find our lives to be more vital, more vibrant, more meaningful. Treat every minute as another contribution to our development as a person, to the people we love and the community that provides the environment for us to live.

As we become more deliberately aware of our time and thinking about distractions, it will become clear that this moment is the time to change. It won't be tomorrow, it can't be yesterday. It has to be now because now is the only time we have.

Chapter 16: Where Do We Start?

Concentrating isn't easy. I mean really concentrating on the task at hand, whether is it an actual physical task, listening to someone speaking to you, staying on track to complete a series of errands or any of hundreds of other responsibilities. It takes genuine effort and desire to not be distracted. When we do focus, the human person is capable of amazing things. That is to say, YOU are capable of amazing things.

Think about the memorable, successful, truly joyful people in our lives whom we either know personally, have met through friends or heard speak at some function. There is a common characteristic we will observe. Most have a very strong sense of purpose and are able to focus on their task, profession, or talent. They have a great capacity for concentrated effort and are not easily distracted. This group includes the teacher who can manage a roomful of restless kids in their classroom and bring a desire to learn to those eager, wandering minds. It's the parent who gets the kids off to school every day, goes through the work day, then gets home and gets everyone through dinner, homework, showers, and makes sure they all get a bit of quality time before bed. Or the parent who skips that late meeting at work to make sure to get to the soccer field to see their son or daughter's big game. Or the grandparent listening intently to the grandchild's description of the first day of kindergarten. But also think of the people who seem to be at almost every turn volunteering, helping, attending. There is truth in the old saying, if you want to get something done, give it to a busy person. Families and communities that are vibrant and healthy work because those involved are intently focused on what needs to be done.

Take time in the next day to do a web search of "volunteer organizations" in your area. You may be quite surprised at how many services are supporting your community based on volunteers. And while volunteering is not the only way to be productive, if you have ever volunteered for an event or project, I am willing to bet that you have a great sense of satisfaction.

The bottom line is that things get done because someone pushed aside the many different choices tugging at their minds and wills and made the conscious choice to do what needed to get done and focus on the primary task. If you think about it, there is probably something you do all the time and don't even consider it a chore, because you know it needs to get done. I can't tell you how many times I said to my own kids in their younger years as I was folding a giant pile of laundry "I'm not doing it because I love doing laundry, I'm doing it because it has to get done."

Parents need to be that example of paying attention, doing the chores that need to be done when they need to be done, being a part of their children's lives, showing with their time and attention that they are important. And although the parent may not see it at the time, the child is seeing what being a parent is all about. While unspoken, it's showing the child that a parent does sacrifice, does do what they can to let the children grow, explore, develop, and then send them on their way...hopefully inspiring them to be that same kind of parent someday.

Think about what we see as evidence a child is growing up. Isn't it when they take on responsibilities, ones with consequences?   From cleaning their room, to doing chores around the house, to the first job for someone other than family, to driving, there are dozens of "events" but they all tell us kids have "grown up" because they are responsible.

Individuals, families, communities, and therefore cultures, survive and thrive when there is general sense of mutual responsibility. And community starts with the home where that sense of responsibility to each family member is established. When that happens, it is a natural progression that when the children leave that household where they shared chores, supported each other, sacrificed for each other, when they enter school and there is a call for a volunteer to help with some project, that child is stepping forward without even thinking about it.

In later years, it's these same active students who often are the backbone of various organizations all the way through college. In later years some will become part of volunteer organizations (fire, EMT, shelters, religious groups, school boards, etc.)

We should be able to see what the benefit is from people around us who live out a sense of purpose and contribution. If we can agree that there is something very pure and true about those around us who we admire, love, support who make a deliberate choice to give of themselves, then we should look at what makes those lives what they are. These kinds of people have made a conscious choice to focus their attention on what is important and not be distracted by that which is not. That choice is not unique to these people. Everyone reading this can be that person. There is nothing genetically different about those productive, positive people. They have simply made the choice to try to not be distracted, to use their time to grow, support, contribute.

And that brings me to the main point of this book. The connected nature of people and what I mentioned earlier in the book regarding being threads in a fabric. We all have a role to play for fabric to stay together.

Chapter 17: Finding a Balance With Our Time

Whatever our role in life, whatever our age, don't we want to do our very best, to contribute?   It's very satisfying to be one of those strong resilient threads in your family or community!

So, let's try to create a picture of what we really want to accomplish with our time. And the answer will be different for each person who is reading this book. We are all at different stages in life with unique situations and responsibilities. Our work, family, relationships...they all add up to a unique life. And that's how it should be. However, I would like to suggest that you consider a very rough formula which you can adjust and mold but with the intention of following the basic premise.

You need time to sleep, eat, commute, work (or go to class), get home. What is left are the hours we can choose to use as best we can. So, if we were to think about a daily routine focusing specifically on the free time, and then consider our immediate primary task and what is right in front of us and our broader primary task related to our stage in life, how we spend those precious hours should start to come into focus.

There is no ABSOLUTE measure because all of our lives are different, our responsibilities are different. But one thing is true. We all know (usually after the fact) when we've burned hours and hours on a useless activity, realizing something much more important didn't get done. That frays the thread. So, let's agree that any measure will be personal, but at the same time, we all also agree you can't get away from our own conscience.

Let's keep it very simple.

ENRICHING   NURTURING   CONTRIBUTING

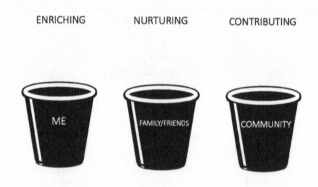

Before I get to how to use this model, for the majority of full time employed adults, work will take up most of our waking hours each day. We work to provide the sustenance we need to live a fruitful and fulfilling life. With that in mind, this model is to track our free hours outside of work responsibilities and be able to see more clearly what we are spending our time on and then, individually, based on our own life situation, make changes that will create better balance fitting to our station in life. But if work hours leave almost no time for family and friends, that should be assessed before the rest of this will have any value.

Some time on "Me"

I always wondered about that rule on the airlines for emergencies and one day, it all made sense. You know the one when the instruction is that in case of an emergency, and you're traveling with a young person, the adult should put their oxygen mask on first before assisting other passengers. The first time I heard it, it sounded incredibly selfish, but then I realized if you're dying of lack of air, you can't help anyone else. And if you're the adult, you need to be lucid to help a child. The same is true more generally, if you're not healthy in every way, you're less able to help others. But, using the airline vernacular, once you get your mask on, you ARE supposed to help others.

So, every person needs to spend some time totally devoted to self-improvement, rest, recreation, and the things that enrich us as people. That's "me" time.

It's part of a healthy life to take a breath, get some exercise, just sit in a quiet spot. It's the **PIES** rule to spend time on our **P**hysical health, **I**ntellectual Stimulation, **E**motional balance and **S**piritual awareness.

Physical health is pretty straightforward, but it will be appropriate and unique for each person. Regular exercise, appropriate for your age and other health factors, has many benefits. Beside the obvious, it also promotes good brain function and a positive attitude. Facing life's challenges is significantly more manageable with a positive attitude.

Intellectual stimulation is remaining curious about the world we live in and accessing the almost unlimited information available to us. Books, magazines, TV, the web can all be used to gain a greater understanding of the world we live in. The classical liberal education used to include a very broad approach to learning. To make good decisions, we need to be informed, but even more than that, we must learn to think critically and reason logically. Schools are at their best when they teach how to think, not what to think. Beyond school, we have access to thousands of sources of information and to the greatest thinkers in history, people who taught others how to think critically. An interesting subject that used to be taught was call rhetoric, which was how to argue a point. The purpose was to learn how to think critically, how to dig into the facts and remove opinion. One key benefit was that two sides could have a reasoned, rational debate on an issue, but based on knowledge and reason.

Emotional balance can include being at peace with yourself and the world. The classic definition of "humility" was not to be a doormat. The Latin root is Humus, which is dirt or ground. Humility meant to be grounded, to be very aware of who you are and aren't. A humble person knows what their abilities are and are not. For a talented golfer, but lousy tennis player, it's a "humble" position to say yes, I'm a very good golfer, but can't play tennis to save my life. This, in turn, means a humble, grounded person knows when to ask for help and when to offer it. Emotional balance allows us to be happy in our own skin, which makes it much easier to handle the many mixed messages we get from the people and society around us.

Spiritual awareness is staying in touch with the reality that everything we have is a gift and for many, that implies a gift giver. We should also to be very aware of all the things in our life that we have to be grateful for. If we woke up today, that's a gift. If we opened our eyes and could see, that's a gift. Having a spouse and children who love you, that's a gift. If you are blessed with truly close friendships, that's a gift. The list goes on, but following the true definition of humility, realizing all these gifts must come from a gift giver, we know we are not the source of all we hold dear and one of the most valuable character traits we can have that grows from this awareness is gratefulness. To be grateful for everything changes how we look at the world. It's easy to see what isn't, the things we don't have, the difficulties we face. But think of it this way, the person who is complaining, they obviously are alive. They are able to think. They can voice an opinion. They can see what should and shouldn't be which inspires action.

The famous motivational speaker Zig Ziglar tells a story of a woman who came to him desperately needing advice. She explained how her employer was absolutely awful, her job was awful, people were against her...the list went on and on. To shorten the story, he asked the woman to make a list of the things that were helpful, good, and positive in her life. It started with her being in good health, that she did have a job, that it provided good pay, provided health benefits, then on to her loving family. Well, you probably already guessed the outcome. When she stopped to think about what was good in her life, she realized it was only her attitude that was negative and the challenges at work, etc. were relatively minor and easily overcome. So, let's start with just being grateful and see where our life goes from there.

Family First, then Friends and immediate responsibilities

When we have ourselves on a good track, then we have to look at our responsibilities. For parents, family must come first, starting in the home and then extending to parents, siblings etc. For these relationships, we absolutely have a unique role no one else can fill in the same way. Think about any of the many movie dramas where, because of some disaster or horrible event, a child is separated from the parent and the heart wrenching scene when they are finally reunited. Even in the midst of whatever disaster has taken place, the child now feels safe in the arms of their parent. It's our job as parents to be that safe and reliable fortress. It is one of the most important things we do as a parent.

By extension, there is the equal responsibility for parents to support each other. Parenting takes a lot of energy, both emotional and physical, so parents need to nurture and revitalize each other for the journey also and be that refuge of safety for each other.

Then we move on to our own parents, the people who dedicated their lives to our benefit. There is the need to be present in their lives and attend to their needs as well. As time goes on, they will almost inevitably go from ones who made sure you were safe, to being totally self-sufficient after we leave the home, to needing more help around their home taking care of household projects and chores and even more serious needs in the final years. And if you have that opportunity to be there to support them in their final years, trust me, that is absolutely one of the things that ONLY a child of a parent can do in that perfectly unique way that no one else can.

There are also siblings and close friends who are that core framework to our lives, the people who are part of all our life events, birthdays, anniversaries, holidays, and more. They surround us in our unique patch of fabric that makes our life work. That's not to say that there aren't challenges and difficulties in any of these situations, but we know for sure that the way it works best is to devote time, love, and patience to keep it all together as best as we can.

Community

Let's also agree that there are times we simply must sacrifice totally for others with no particular benefit to ourselves, just because it's the right thing to do. Community starts with where you live as well as who you come in contact with, but also can include associations and groups that do good work and support ideals important to a healthy society. At times it can be totally random, like stopping to help a stranger with a flat tire or help with directions. Other times it will be a planned and deliberate effort to volunteer for an organization... that's "them" time. There are so many places where we can pitch in and for small towns in particular, volunteers are needed for many organizations to run at all.

How any particular person can contribute will vary depending on life circumstance. For those in good health and with time available, getting involved in any number of community projects might be an option. For some not able to get out, it might be to reach out with a call, email, or letter to a person who just needs a kind ear. There are wonderful organizations that can benefit from financial support and outreach. It will depend on a person's situation, where they can contribute.

Tracking our Time

So back to the buckets. You will now have a tool to track your progress through the day, week, month. Yes, buckets are bit much, so get three plastic cups and a bag of marbles, or even use coins. Write the categories on each and use one marble or coin per hour of time you have spent that day in each category.
Remember, this isn't meant to put on the mantle for the world to see. This is a self-tracking tool meant for you to take your own measure and decide what needs to be changed.

Assuming a fairly accurate count on the hours, it becomes visually clear as our day, week, and month progresses how we are spending our time. Five hours a night on mindless video games fills the "me" bucket up pretty quickly. Doing many hours of community service but neglecting the family fills up the "community" bucket out of proportion. Doing nothing for self-improvement or self-enrichment weakens your ability to support others. Never doing anything out of total self sacrifice keeps us detached from the community we live in.

Each person, based on their own life situation, will have different hours spent in each area. A person recovering from illness will rightly have much more focus on "me," on healing, on recovery. Getting out of the house may be difficult, but might it be possible to add to "family" time and make a call to a family member or friend who may need a kind ear?

For young parents, the "family" bucket will likely be the most full almost every week, but young parents in particular really need some "me" time in the schedule to refresh and recharge. The goal is not to end up with too many days going by and no "me" time at all. Retired folks... well, if you are healthy and able bodied, there are many ways your family and community would benefit from your wisdom and life experience.

The combinations are endless and no one else knows your life and responsibilities like you do. However, this model only works if you are truly honest in tracking time each day and only you can look back at a week and month and know you are doing your best to keep in balance. But if we can be mindful, be aware, we can start to see very clearly what things are pulling us away from keeping some balance in our lives.

The purpose is to give ourselves permission to enjoy some down time, to recognize and accept our responsibilities to family and friends, and remember that there are times we must forget ourselves and look outward.

Throughout a week, a month, a year, that mix will move and adjust. Life is not linear and it often comes at us with no intention whatsoever of sticking to a formula. You may suddenly find yourself giving up virtually all your free time after work to help out with a school or community project or tending to a relative who is sick or recovering from an injury. You may be at a point in life where the accumulated stresses of life can only be managed with greater hours of quiet and rest. There isn't one formula for all. Each mix of hours will balance a little differently. But with more of us paying attention, I believe we will see families and communities changing.

If we look at distraction for what it is, if we look at the responsibilities right in front of us as OUR responsibilities and we choose to own them, we can't help but grow into a strong, vibrant, vital thread in the fabric of life. With a very clear primary task and distractions under control, we will leave a legacy of a person who grew our gifts and talents, a person who nurtured and loved our family and a community enriched by our contribution and everyone who comes into contact with us being thankful that we were in their lives.

"Consult not your fears but your hopes and your dreams. Think not of your frustrations, but about your unfulfilled potential. Concern yourself not with what you tried and failed in, but with what is still possible for you to do."
Pope John XXIII

Made in United States
North Haven, CT
01 March 2023

33342832R00071